The Automotive Sale Process

The Automotive Sale Process

The Nine Stages to the Sale

Gilton Huggett

Copyright © 2023 by Gilton Huggett All rights reserved.

No part of this publication may be reproduced, stored in a retrieval system, or transmitted in any form or by any means, electronic, mechanical, photocopying, recording, scanning, or otherwise, without the prior written permission of the author.

Limit of Liability/Disclaimer of Warranty: This publication is designed to provide accurate and authoritative information in regard to the subject matter covered. It is sold with the understanding that neither the author nor the publisher is engaged in rendering legal, investment, accounting or other professional services. While the publisher and author have used their best efforts in preparing this book, they make no representations or warranties with respect to the accuracy or completeness of the contents of this book and specifically disclaim any implied warranties of merchantability or fitness for a particular purpose. No warranty may be created or extended by sales representatives or written sales materials. The advice and strategies contained herein may not be suitable for your situation. You should consult with a professional when appropriate. Neither the publisher nor the author shall be liable for any loss of profit or any other commercial damages, including but not limited to special, incidental, consequential, personal, or other damages.

The Automotive Sale Process

Gilton Huggett

ISBN: 979-8-9877312-0-8

Printed in the United States of America

Table of Contents

Chapter One 1
Meet and Greet *1*

Chapter Two 4
Needs Assessment *4*

Chapter Three 8
The Vehicle Presentation *8*

Chapter Four 12
Test Drive *12*

Chapter Five 16
Trial Close *16*

Chapter Six 20
Trade Evaluation *20*

Chapter Seven 24

Negotiate and Close *24*

Chapter Eight 30

Business Office Visit *30*

Chapter Nine 34

Special Delivery *34*

About the Author . 39

Introduction

This book covers various strategies for developing an efficient career in the Automotive Sales Industry. In my work as a Sales Consultant, I utilize the following steps. Most Dealerships use similar steps but I modified them based on my understanding and experience. There is no need to change the wheel, but I will apply a unique philosophy to these basic concepts. In this book, I will use the term "stage" instead of "step" to distinguish myself. My goal is to encourage people to enter the industry and make a difference in people's lives.

Historically society has a negative connotation of the automotive sales industry. Since the creation of the Internet, business is much more transparent than in the past. Most information such as pricing, videos, and window stickers are available on the manufacturers' websites, third-party sites, and dealerships' websites. Most customers come to the dealership very educated about the process, so it is vital for Sales Consultants to be knowledgeable about their products. If you are unable to answer questions and explain the features and benefits of the vehicles, you are going to lose credibility. Studying the business very well is critical for success, as understanding the features and benefits of the vehicle you are selling compared to the competition. If you can illustrate the advantages your vehicles have compare to the competition, you can prevent your customer from going to another dealership.

The steps to automotive sales will not be a straight line but will involve obstacles, rewards, and awards. Society often has a negative view of the automotive sales industry. In my experience, however, it is very empowering to help people make a decision that is sometimes the first large purchase of their lives.

The Automotive Sale Process

Chapter One

Meet and Greet

The First stage of the automotive process is the meet and greet. The first impression will determine whether a customer is going to buy from you. The way the sales consultant dresses or speaks will be an essential factor. Because of that, you have to prepare for many rejections. However, do not take it personally; it is often a defense mechanism. The most common response from a customer will be, "I am just looking." You can easily overcome this by saying, "Looking for Parts, Service, or Sales?" Some people may laugh, relax a little, and tell you what they are looking for. The smart thing to do is, let them sit at your desk and ask simple questions like, "How is the weather today?" or

Gilton Huggett

"Do you live or work in the area?" The goal is to make the customer feel comfortable. Bear in mind there are 6.9 billion individuals in the world with 6.9 billion personalities so one strategy is not going to work for everyone. Nevertheless, having a strategy is better than letting the customer pass you and work with someone else.

This stage is like baseball: even the best hitter will get out many times. The highest-paid players hit an average of .300, meaning 70% of the time they are out. However, 30% of the time they hit the ball. Failure is a part of the process, but you cannot let one person spoil your parade. You have to be as enthusiastic about person #10 as you were about the first nine people, even if each of those nine people said no.

The Automotive Sale Process

Because enthusiasm is critical in this stage of the process, your body language and facial expressions are vital for success. I highly recommend having clean clothing, nice grooming, and shining shoes. Avoid carrying a cup of coffee, a bottle of water, or a cigarette in your hand when greeting customers to optimize professionalism. Looking professional is essential for success in this stage. Once you've made an excellent first impression, the next chapter of this book will discuss needs assessment.

Chapter Two

Needs Assessment

The goal of the second stage of the process, the Needs Assessment, is to figure out what the customers are looking for. It is imperative to ask open-ended questions to get the customer to elaborate on the features and benefits of the right vehicle to select for them. The consequences faced by putting the customers in the wrong car could be detrimental to the transaction. Most salespeople may be trying to land the customer on a car with a spiff, which will be beneficial for a nice commission from a Sales Consultant's perspective, but will not be beneficial to the customer's needs. For instance,

The Automotive Sale Process

some salespeople will have a customer test drive the most expensive car in the dealership and the customer needs the most affordable. You have to be empathetic to the customers' needs.

Put yourself in the customer's shoes: if you were buying a car, you would not want anyone to let you buy something that is not in your budget or you did not like. The successful salesperson does what the unsuccessful salesperson refuses to do: the right thing. Doing the right thing by considering the customer's needs will make the process goes smoothly. If you test drive five cars, then the customers will be overwhelmed and will not be prepared to make a decision. After multiple test drives, the customer is going to say, "I need to think about it." Most customers who say this will then leave your dealership to go to another dealership, where another salesperson will narrow them down to the right vehicle and close the sale. It will be very frustrating for the salesperson to follow up the next day and for the customer to say, "We bought another car, thanks for your time yesterday." If a proper needs assessment was implemented, then the customer will be able to decide on the spot.

Losing a sale is very painful when you put your blood, sweat, and tears into it, but sometimes your poor decisions in the Needs Assessment contributed to the loss from the start. This is one of the most important stages in the sales process because it is often where sales are gained or lost. Ask the right questions

The Automotive Sale Process

and you can put the customer in the right car. If you can sit the customers down and write the information on paper, then get the appropriate vehicle that fits the customer's desires and needs, the process would be simpler. After you've found the appropriate vehicle, the next chapter will discuss the vehicle presentation.

Chapter Three

The Vehicle Presentation

The third stage of the process is vehicle presentation. After narrowing down which vehicle best serves the customer, you must go outside for the appropriate vehicle, pull it up, and review the vehicle. Tailoring the presentation to the customer's requirements will be the most effective approach. You do not want to sound like a pre-recorded third-party vehicle review video. Remember the concepts that were most important to the customer and go over the specific features and benefits of the technology that they said they are interested in. Open the driver's door, the back passenger

The Automotive Sale Process

door, and the trunk. Review trunk versatility and show them where the spare tire is, and the tools to change the tire in an emergency. If seats can fold down, show the customer that there is space for a bicycle or long surfboards in the trunk with the back seat folded down. At the back door, illustrate legroom in the back seats and show the anchors for child seats if children are going to be in the car.

At the front door, allow the customer sit down and adjust the driver's seat and steering to their delight. Review the turn signal stalk, wiper stalk, and light switch, and demonstrate how to adjust interior and exterior mirrors. Pair up the customer's smartphone to review Apple Car Play or Android Auto if applicable. Illustrate to them how to use the voice command button on the steering wheel for their podcast or app songs network, which will demonstrate the efficiency of the sound system and functionality of the manufacturers' system. The more effectively the customer can utilize the interior features, the more enthusiastic they will be toward the vehicle.

If they are very comfortable with everything, it is imperative to proceed immediately to the test drive. Never leave the presentation stage and then go to negotiation, which is the most common strategy today. As the old saying goes, "The feel of the wheel is the key to the deal." Customers make decisions emotionally and then rationalize logically why they made the decision. If you do not go to the test drive phase, then it is more of a

The Automotive Sale Process

transactional selling process instead of a consultative approach. The customer's buying experience will be poor and customer review scores will be very low. The next chapter will discuss the principles of the test drive.

Chapter Four

Test Drive

The fourth stage of the process is the test drive. The sales consultant should start driving first and then change over with the customer at the predetermined change point. (Make sure the change point is a safe area such as a shopping center, gas station, etc. Never pull over on a highway or busy main road.) While the sales consultant is driving, try to demonstrate acceleration by accelerating on an entrance ramp of the highway, and before demonstrating braking, tell the customer, "Hang tight, I am going to be braking the car now." Show the customer all safety features such as adaptive

The Automotive Sale Process

cruise control, lane departure warning, blind spot monitoring, and smart city brakes. Turn on the adaptive cruise control, set the car lengths, and show the customer how the car automatically stops and returns to the set speed you were driving.

Intentionally try to deviate from the lane without turning on the turn signal and let the customer listen to the lane departure warning. Turn on the turn signal when you are passing another vehicle for the blind spot warning sound to be alerted. Then try to get close to the car ahead of you without utilizing the brakes and illustrate how the car will stop automatically with a smart city brake. After illustrating all the safety features and driving dynamics. Drive the vehicle into a shopping center, if a mirror is available, park close to the mirror, so customers can see the vehicle in the mirror. This could draw the customer's attention to the beautiful color and exterior design of the vehicle.

As you change over to the customer driving, limit talking to giving them directions back to the dealership. The quieter the customer is during the driving experience the more likely they are going to develop an emotional attachment to the vehicle and make a valid decision at the end of the test drive. Your goal is to increase the emotional side of the customer's emotional-to-logical ratio. If the emotional ratio is about 70% and the logical ratio is 30%, the chance of gaining a sale is very high. In contrast, if the customers' emotional ratio is 30% and the logical ratio is 70%, the

The Automotive Sale Process

chance of gaining sales is very low. The next chapter will review some strategies to evaluate the customers' temperature toward the transaction.

Chapter Five

Trial Close

The fifth stage of the process is Trial Close. The goal of this stage is to evaluate the customers' temperature towards making the decision. Emotional to logical ratio will be in effect to determine the outcome. You must ask open-ended questions for the customer to elaborate, on whether they are going to proceed with the transaction or move in a different direction. The two most commonly asked questions are:

1. "Is there anything you dislike about the vehicle thus far?"
2. "How are you feeling about the vehicle thus far?"

The Automotive Sale Process

Note well, never ask, "How are you thinking about the vehicle thus far?" Since "I am going to think about it" is the most commonly used objection for the customer at this stage. Do not use the word "thinking" period. Do not set yourself up for objection.

Asking the first two questions above will lead the customer to consider their feelings towards the vehicle. When asked if there's anything they dislike about the vehicle, the customer will respond one of two ways:

- Best Case Scenario: "No, I didn't see anything I dislike about the vehicle, could we go in and evaluate the numbers?"
- Worst Case Scenario: "I did not like the acceleration, it is underpowered, the

seats are uncomfortable, and my head is hitting the roof."

When asked how they are feeling about the vehicle, the customer could respond:

- Best Case Scenario: "I have driven five different brands, and this vehicle has been the most exceptional thus far. What's the next step?"
- Worst Case Scenario: "I am very sorry, this vehicle is too advanced for me, and I do not like all this technology."

The best practice is to ask these questions in the vehicle at the end of the test drive, if the answers were the worst-case scenario answers, the chances of getting the sale would be very low. In contrast, if the answers were the best-

The Automotive Sale Process

case scenario, the chance of selling the vehicle will be high. In automotive sales, nothing is guaranteed because we could encounter trade objections or high-interest rates for some of these best-case scenarios customers that could prevent a sale. The next Chapter will discuss trade evaluation.

Chapter Six

Trade Evaluation

The Sixth stage of the process is Trade Evaluation. Just because the best-case scenarios customers said they are ready to move forward, the trade will play a vital role for them to complete the transaction. Once you go inside to your desk, the first question you will ask is. "Are you going to be trading a vehicle or just adding to your fleet?" If they said "Yes, I do have a Trade." You should then ask them, "Do you own it outright or still owe money on it?" If they own it outright, you just want to confirm they brought the title with them. Having a title with them is a good prognosis, meaning they

The Automotive Sale Process

are prepared to go ahead if everything is aligned correctly. In contrast, if they still owe money on the vehicle, you must confirm which bank the vehicle is financed through and call the bank to get the ten-day payoff. Most dealerships have trade evaluation sheets; best practice is the write the ten-day payoff value down on the sheet.

After confirming the availability of the title or writing down the ten-day payoff of the vehicle, you must bring the customer with you to look at the trade. If the dealership has an appraisal sheet, put the sheet on a clipboard, there will be questions on the sheet you could ask the customer about the vehicle as you do a walk-around.

Gilton Huggett

First, write down the Vehicle Identification Number, which will be easily found in the most common location, the lower left corner of the windshield. If it is blocked then check the driver's door jamb. Second, ask the customer to start the car and read the mileage off the odometer, check to see if you see the check engine light on or the tire pressure sign blinking. Then open all four doors, and evaluate for scratches and door dings. If you find scratches and door dings, be sure you ask the customer, "What happened here?" Take a dime to measure the treads in all four tires, check the windshield for cracks, and check the front and rear bumpers to see if the vehicle may have been involved in an accident.

The Automotive Sale Process

On the appraisal sheet, one of the questions to ask is, "Has the vehicle been involved in an accident?" After completing all questions on the sheet, go back to your desk and ask the customer if they did any research or had an offer for their vehicle. If they say yes then ask them to write the offer on the appraisal sheet. If not, the next step is to go to the Used Car Manager or Used Car Director. Give them the appraisal sheet and the keys. They will do a quick reading of the sheet and then go outside to do their evaluation and provide a value for the trade. Once this is accomplished, the next Chapter will discuss the Negotiate and Close.

Chapter Seven

Negotiate and Close

The Seventh stage of the process is Negotiate and Close. While the Used Car Director is evaluating the vehicle, the best practice for this stage is to have a guest sheet. You must ask relevant questions in this stage to be very efficient, do not miss any questions. You are serving as an advocate for the customer, so be sure to ask every relevant question:

1. "Whose name is the vehicle going to be titled under?"
2. "Could you spell your last name please?"
3. "Could you spell your first name please?"

The Automotive Sale Process

4. "What is the physical address the vehicle will be registered with?"
5. "What is the best contact number for you?"
6. "What is your email address?"
7. "Are you going to be financing or paying cash?"
8. If financing, "What terms would you like to finance for?"
9. "How much down payment?"
10. "What is your credit rating?" (If the customer is unclear, ask on a scale of one to 10. 10 being excellent, 7 average, or three below average.)
11. "If terms and figures are agreeable are you in a position to purchase now?"

Gilton Huggett

In the best-case scenario, customers will say yes. In contrast, worst-case scenario customers will say no. After asking all the questions and completing the guest sheet, bring it to the Sales desk. The management team is going to work in a symbiotic approach to provide a best-case scenario for the transaction to work. They are going to create a purchase agreement that will include:

- Manufacturer's Suggested Retail Price
- Sale price
- Taxes
- Title
- Fees
- Trade Value
- Payoff

The Automotive Sale Process

- Finance Terms
- Monthly Payments
- Down Payments

After it is printed, you present it to the customer. The best practice is to go over the numbers, be quiet, and leave the pen at the signature line. Silence is vital since whoever speaks first will lose. Best-case scenario customers will take the pen and sign or in the worst-case scenario, the customer will want to negotiate. It is only fitting since we are in the negotiating stage most people are going to negotiate. About 10% of the customers will sign immediately, but 90% of customers will want to negotiate.

The most common negotiation topic will be the trade. Since there are several third-party sites, customers could type in their Vehicle Identification Number and Mileage to get an estimate of what their vehicle is worth before arriving at the dealership, and they often come with a copy of estimated values in their pockets. However, customers occasionally make mistakes in their research like entering the wrong odometer mileage or selecting "excellent condition" or the retail value instead of the trade-in value. The best practice is to look at the printout correctly, to make sure all information matches correctly. If you did an efficient trade appraisal sheet, the customer's objection can be easily overcome. If the customer says, "I saw on this third-party site that this vehicle is worth much more than you are offering," then you say, "Let's review the trade appraisal sheet. You

The Automotive Sale Process

have a cracked windshield, we have to replace your four tires, your check engine light is on, and your front bumper needs to be replaced. All those deficiencies are contributing to why we are lower than the third party offer."

After you justify your offer with facts, most customers will sign the paperwork and you will close the transaction. Closing the transaction is like making a football touchdown: it is a very exciting phase of the transaction. Once the customer signs the purchase agreement sheet, the next Chapter is the Business Office Visit.

Chapter Eight

Business Office Visit

The Eighth stage of the process is the Business Office Visit. When the customer signs the purchase agreement sheet, the Business Office Paperwork will be started. Ask customers for their driver's licenses and insurance. The first step is to complete the credit application, for the best results, the sales consultant should write this out manually for the customer. Ask the questions and fill in the blanks. The rationale is if the information is not written clearly, you do not understand what the customers wrote, and the Business Manager asks you, then the process will be slowed down. Everyone

The Automotive Sale Process

comprehends their own handwriting so the answer will be easy to give.

Once the credit application is complete, the customer will sign the credit application sheet and privacy statement. The next step is to take a Vehicle Identification Number verification sheet, go to the vehicle the customer is purchasing, and write the Vehicle Identification Number and the Mileage on the vehicle. Then complete the We Owe sheet, make sure you confirm with the customer the miles on the vehicle and that you do not owe them anything but truly exceptional customer service. Make sure they sign the Vehicle Identification Number verification sheet and we owe sheet. Afterward, make a copy of the driver's license and Insurance. Depending on the dealership you are going to be working at, there will be a different folder for the Pre-Owned Vehicle compared to the New Vehicle. Make sure you select the correct folder. On the back of the folder is where you will write information for the ten-day payoff of the vehicle.

Once you complete all required paperwork, have the Desk Manager approve it, then bring the folder to the Business Office. If it is a Pre-Owned Vehicle, additional paperwork will be needed for the folder, and you must put in Car Fax, Recall sheet, As-Is sheet and Certified Paperwork for the Certified Pre-Owned vehicles.

While the customer waits for the Business Office, to reduce tension and anxiety, take them to your Parts and Service Department for a tour

The Automotive Sale Process

of the dealership. Offer them refreshments and snacks if possible. Never leave them alone because this is a perfect time for building rapport with them. Once the Business Manager comes to escort them to the Business Office, this will be a good time for you to bring the vehicle for detail. The Final Stage of the transaction begins Special Delivery. The next Chapter will discuss the Special Delivery.

Chapter Nine

Special Delivery

The Ninth stage of the process is Special Delivery. Once the Business Manager escorts the customers to the Business Office. It is time to bring the vehicle they are purchasing to the Detail Department. First, put a full tank of gas in the vehicle and hand the vehicle off to the detail team. Ask the Detail team for a potential estimated time the vehicle will be ready. Get the books (warranty and owner's manual) for the vehicle and the second key for the vehicle. If the Business Office concludes before the detail team completes the vehicle, then there is time for you to review the books with customers. Show them

The Automotive Sale Process

the Owner's Manual and important chapters they need to review to enhance the ownership experience. Review the Warranty Book to distinguish between the Basic and Powertrain expiration time period for the vehicle. Make sure to explain what is covered and what is not covered. Also, let them save the roadside assistance phone number in their cell phone.

After reviewing the books, ask the Sales desk for the temporary tag for the vehicle. The best practice is to bring the temporary tag back to the make ready Department, and install the temporary tag before you return to the delivery area. Check the vehicle after the detail team finishes making sure there are no scratches or door dings. If you see any residual water on the vehicle, take a clean towel to dry it. Check for dust on the dashboard; if dust still exists, wipe it off with a damp cloth. Check the floor mats to make sure they are anchored properly. Lift to make sure no dirt is under the mats. Make sure the tire pressure light is not on, and test the tire pressure of the vehicle to make sure the values match what is in the door jamb. Drive the vehicle back to the Delivery area. The best practice is to reverse the vehicle in the Delivery area, so they will have an easy exit once you complete the review of the features and benefits.

Once you bring the car around, ask the customers to do a walk-around to make sure they did not see any scratches or door dings. This is a good practice because if they went to a supermarket and get a door ding they cannot

The Automotive Sale Process

say we sold the car like that. Sit on the passenger side and review with the customer, how to set their ideal seating position, steering wheel position, and left and right exterior mirror positions. Explain how to preset their favorite radio stations, pair their cell phone, and set the AC and heat systems. Make sure they know how to open the gas tank, hood, and trunk from the inside. The best practice is to tailor the presentation to the items that are most important for the customers.

After they are comfortable with the features. The best practice is to take pictures with customers to express your gratitude for their business. Let them know that if they have any questions after they leave today, you will be just a phone call away. In addition, if they want to come back for another review session, they could schedule a date or time. After the customer leaves the dealership, if it is early in the day, give them a two-hour grace period, and call them to tell them thanks for their business. Send a thank you email and attach one of your business cards and a brochure of the service schedule. Follow up with customers as frequently as possible using their preferred communication method.

These are my nine stages of the automotive sales process. Each dealership or customer will be slightly different. My overall advice is to tailor the process to the customer because silver and gold will vanish away but exceptional customer service will never decay.

About the Author

Gilton Huggett is a 15-year veteran Sales Consultant at Russell and Smith Mazda in Houston, Texas. He has won Salesperson of the Month fifty-six times and Salesperson of the year eight times. He was Mazda Elite Master Certified Sales Consultant 2012 through 2017 and the 2013 Extra Mile award winner for Russell and Smith Mazda. Before pursuing a

Gilton Huggett

career in the Automotive Sales Industry, Gilton's journey was a struggle.

First, he went to City College of New York, and was accepted into the Engineering Program but could not pass Linear Algebra. After failing this course three times, he had to withdraw from the program. Gilton took two years off from College due to severe depression and lost focus. Then, he went to Bronx Community College where he did well in the prerequisites for the Nursing program (Microbiology, Anatomy, and physiology). Was accepted into the Nursing program. First Semester he failed hand washing, and he had to withdraw from the program. The second time around failed Bed Making and the third time around failed Bed Making and had to leave the program.

The Automotive Sale Process

On June 01, 2000, Gilton graduated from Lehman College with a 3.43 GPA cum laude in Public Health, graduating third in his class. He anticipated that he would have served as a great Candidate for a job. He participated in 63 Interviews and went zero for 63. Everyone said the same thing. "Your credentials are great but your Jamaican accent is not refined enough for our Job opening." He decided to go to Sint Eustatius School of Medicine and graduated in two years but he could not pass the Medical Boards to advance to Clinical Rotations.

Gilton moved to Houston, Texas, and went to John Eagle Honda for an interview because they had an opening for Car Sales Consultant. After talking to the sales Manager for five minutes, the manager said, "I don't want to waste your time and my time, with your horrific Jamaican accent you will not make it in the car business. Check Walmart up the road, they are looking for someone to stock shelves at night." After Gilton walk through the door, he got a call from a lady who was doing an Automotive Sales training and recruiting program. She trained him for three days and took him to Russell & Smith Auto Group for an Interview. After going zero for 64 in interviews, the Russell and Smith Auto Group said yes, and he was very shocked to hear yes. So he promised them that he would not disappoint them, He would be the first to work every day and last to leave.

Because he had failed and been rejected so often, despite his horrific Jamaican accent,

The Automotive Sale Process

Gilton's character made him a remarkable candidate for an Automotive Sales Consultant. The rationale being, even if the first customer hangs up the phone on him, he will be just as enthusiastic about the next call as the previous call. If someone says no, they are not going to buy the car, he will not take it personally, because he is the master of rejection. He has flourished and has an illustrious career in the Automotive Sales Industry and wrote this book to inspire people who may be contemplating pursuing this career.

www.ingramcontent.com/pod-product-compliance
Lightning Source LLC
Chambersburg PA
CBHW070552090426
42735CB00013B/3158